CLIMATE CHANGE
Wildfires

By Clinton Williams

PORMPURAAW LAND AND SEA MANAGEMENT

We respect and honour Aboriginal and Torres Strait Islander Elders past, present and future. We acknowledge the stories, traditions and living cultures of Aboriginal and Torres Strait Islander peoples on this land and commit to building a brighter future together.

Library For All Ltd.

What is Climate Change?

Climate change means long-term changes in weather, like temperature and rainfall, caused mostly by human activities. These activities include burning fossil fuels, cutting down forests, and industrial processes, which increase greenhouse gases and trap heat in the atmosphere.

The Earth's temperature and weather patterns are changing.

How does climate change affect fires?

Climate change makes places hotter and drier, which helps fires start and spread more easily. Higher temperatures dry out plants, making them more likely to catch fire. Changes in rainfall can also cause long droughts, increasing fire risk.

Climate change causes dry plants, stronger winds, and more lightning strikes.

Indigenous Perspectives

Traditional signs a fire is coming

Indigenous knowledge includes observing natural signs like animal behaviour, plant conditions, smells or sounds that indicate a fire might be near. Rangers might see land animals like wallabies, kangaroos and feral pigs fleeing. Eagles and hawks will fly high in the sky, circling an area waiting for frogs, little animals and insects who are escaping the fire.

Rangers observe the difference in the colour of smoke. Dark smoke will indicate that there is a hot burn and that it might include areas such as woodlands, and trees such as paperbark. Light smoke will indicate that the fire is cooler and that the fire is more likely to be grassland.

Fire's effects on the land and community

Fires can change the makeup and structure of local ecosystems. Animals may lose their habitats and food sources. Water sources can get contaminated with ash and debris. Some plants and animals are adapted to fire and can recover quickly, while others struggle. This disruption can lead to long-term changes.

Fires can destroy plants, leaving the land bare and increasing erosion risk.

Pormpuraaw Community Views

The number of fires at Pormpuraaw varies each year, but the community is careful to monitor and manage risk. Fires can damage vegetation, affect wildlife, harm homes and cultural sites, and disrupt community life.

Community members also share stories of resilience and recovery, showing how traditional knowledge helps save lives and protect the environment. These stories highlight the importance of respecting natural cycles.

Communities like Pormpuraaw use controlled pre-burning, called 'cool burns', to reduce fuel loads and prevent larger fires. Pormpuraaw rangers have been very successful with their cool burns, almost eliminating large, out of control wildfires over the last few years.

Cool Burns vs Hot Burns

Cool burns are low-intensity fires conducted under controlled conditions to reduce fuel loads and manage the landscape. They are usually done during cooler, wetter periods to minimise risk and promote healthy ecosystems.

Cool burns done by the Pormpuraaw Rangers give insects and animals time to move safely away from the fire, while hot burns don't give them enough time to escape.

How does pre-burning help fire prevention?

Hot burns are high-intensity fires that occur during hot, dry weather. Their burn causes significant damage to the environment, infrastructure, and communities. Hot burns can destroy large areas of vegetation, kill wildlife, and damage soil. They can lead to erosion and water contamination and pose significant risks to human life and property.

Cool burns reduce the amount of dry vegetation, or fuel, available for wildfires, making it harder for large fires to start and spread. They also promote biodiversity by encouraging germination of fire-adapted plants.

Cool Burning

Traditional cool burn practices

A cool burn is performed by starting 5-10 small, controlled fires. Removing vegetation creates fire breaks, so that bigger wildfires do not get out of control. Hot fires will burn and destroy everything they pass. You will know a cool burn area because the trees will stay alive, you will see green canopies and you will see the black (carbon) burn marks only about half way up the larger trees.

Modern scientific research also supports using cool burns for effective fire management. Studies show that regular cool burns can reduce the r sk of large, destructive wildfires and help maintain healthy ecosystems. Climate change makes it harder to do cool burns safely, however. Unpredictable weather can narrow the window of time for safe burns.

Preparation Strategies – Indigenous Perspectives

Preparing for fire season in Pormpurraw includes creating firebreaks, reducing fuel loads through controlled burns, and developing emergency plans. Education and community engagement are vital to ensure everyone knows how to stay safe and protect their property.

12

When a fire warning is issued, communities activate their emergency plans.

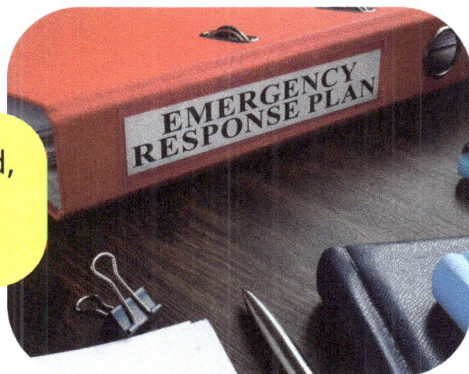

Local rangers know that fire season is beginning when they start feeling the warmer SE wind that comes off the country. Cooler winds coming from the sea usually indicate that it is not yet wildfire season.

DID YOU KNOW?

Cool burns and traditional knowledge of local fire behaviour are integrated into modern fire management.

Modern Science Insights

Fire preparation is important. Experts recommend creating cleared space and access routes around homes and having an emergency kit and evacuation plan ready. Regularly updating and practicing these plans is essential.

How does climate change affect fire preparation?

Climate change requires more proactive and adaptive fire preparation strategies. This includes increased weather monitoring, investing in fire-resistant infrastructure, and enhancing community awareness and readiness. Safety measures include following evacuation orders, protecting homes with fire-resistant materials, and using fire shelters. Community coordination and clear communication are vital to ensuring everyone's safety.

Recovery efforts involve restoring damaged ecosystems, replanting vegetation, and supporting affected communities.

Traditional knowledge and fire recovery

Pormpuraaw supports the natural regrowth cycle after a fire, rather than active revegetation. Wildfires support natural regrowth in a few ways:

1 Nutrient cycling: fires release nutrients like nitrogen, phosphorus, and potassium into the soil, making them available for plant growth.

2 Germination: certain plants have seeds that require fire's heat or smoke to geminate. They're called fire-adapted species.

3 Habitat restoration: fires create open spaces that benefit certain wildlife and promote habitat diversity and biodiversity.

4 Control of pests and diseases: fire reduces populations of pests and pathogens, helping control the spread of diseases and damage to plants.

5 Reduction of competition: Fires clear dense underbrush, reducing competition for sunlight, water and nutrients, allowing new plants to thrive.

6 Soil improvement: Heat from fires Heat from fires improves soil structure and reduces harmful pathogens, creating a favorable environment for new growth.

7 So fires are important for the natural cycle of country but very hot, out of control wildfires are not good for people or country.

Fires can create a mix of burned and unburned areas, supporting different species.

Modern Science Insights

Fire recovery

Climate change can slow recovery by creating less favourable conditions for regrowth, like prolonged droughts and increased temperatures. This can lead to long-term ecological impacts and challenges for land management.

DID YOU KNOW?

Over time, fire-adapted plants may thrive, and new growth can provide food and shelter for wild ife. Building resilience to future fires through improved land management is important.

Cultural Impacts of Fires

Fires can threaten sacred sites, traditional lands, and cultural practices. Losing these places can deeply affect community identity and heritage. Protection includes creating firebreaks, monitoring fire risk, and involving community members in safeguarding these areas.

Modern science perspectives

Climate change increases the risk of damage to cultural sites from fires, floods, and other extreme weather.

It also affects traditional practices that rely on predictable environmental conditions.

Experts use field surveys, mapping, and historical research to identify and protect cultural heritage sites. They also work with local communities to develop fire management plans that include cultural values.

HOW CAN WE HELP?

Properly dispose of and extinguish campfires and cigarettes.

Create and maintain defensible clear pace around your home.

Participate in community fire preparedness and education programs.

Advocate for the inclusion of traditional knowledge in fire management policies. Community engagement and policy advocacy are also important.

Reducing greenhouse gas emissions, supporting renewable energy initiatives, and promoting sustainable land use practices.

23

Photo Credits

Page	Attribution
Cover	Stu Shaw/Shutterstock.com
Page 2	Oliverdelahaye/Shutterstock.com
Page 3	SherSS/Shutterstock.com
Page 4	© Library For All
Page 5	Unsplash Licence/Unsplash.com
Page 6	Daria Nipot/Shutterstock.com
Page 7	Photo courtesy of the Queensland Indigenous Land and Sea Ranger Program.
Page 8	Photo courtesy of the Queensland Indigenous Land and Sea Ranger Program.
Page 9	tomertu/Shutterstock.com
Page 10–11	Philip Game / Alamy Stock Photo
Page 12	Photo courtesy of the Queensland Indigenous Land and Sea Ranger Program.
Page 13	Vitalii Vodolazskyi/Shutterstock.com
Page 14	© Library For All
Page 15	© Library For All
Page 18 (all)	© Library For All
Page 19	Unsplash Licence/Unsplash.com
Page 20	Photo courtesy of the Queensland Indigenous Land and Sea Ranger Program.
Page 21	Photo courtesy of the Queensland Indigenous Land and Sea Ranger Program.
Page 22	Unsplash Licence/Unsplash.com
Page 23 (above)	Photo courtesy of the Queensland Indigenous Land and Sea Ranger Program.
Page 23 (below)	Unsplash Licence/Unsplash.com

You can use these questions to talk about this book with your family, friends and teachers.

What did you learn from this book?

Describe this book in one word. Funny? Scary? Colourful? Interesting?

How did this book make you feel when you finished reading it?

What was your favourite part of this book?

Download the Library For All Reader app from libraryforall.org

Queensland Indigenous Land and Sea Ranger Program

The Queensland Indigenous Land and Sea Ranger Program collaborates with First Nations communities to protect and care for land and sea Country. With over 200 rangers, the program shares cultural knowledge, engages in community education, and leads youth programs like the Junior Ranger initiative, fostering a strong connection to Country and Culture.

Clinton Williams is a Ranger of the Pormpuraaw community.

Darwin

NORTHERN
TERRITORY

QUEENSLAND

WESTERN
AUSTRALIA

SOUTH
AUSTRALIA

Brisbane

NEW SOUTH
WALES

Perth

Adelaide

ACT

Sydney

VICTORIA

Canberra

Melbourne

TASMANIA

Hobart

Our Yarning

The Our Yarning collection aligns with the Australian Curriculum through the Cross-Curriculum Priorities — Aboriginal and Torres Strait Islander Histories and Cultures. The collection provides an authentic opportunity for learning and embedding Aboriginal and Torres Strait Islander perspectives because it is written by Aboriginal and Torres Strait Islander people.

We know that children learn better, and enjoy reading more, when they see themselves in the stories, characters and illustrations of the books they read.

To download the app, visit the Google Play Store or Apple Store and search 'Our Yarning'.

librariesforall.org

You're reading Upper Primary

Learner – Beginner readers

Start your reading journey with short words, big ideas and plenty of pictures.

Level 1 – Rising readers

Raise your reading level with more words, simple sentences and exciting images.

Level 2 – Eager readers

Enjoy your reading time with familiar words, but complex sentences.

Level 3 – Progressing readers

Develop your reading skills with creative stories and some challenging vocabulary.

Level 4 – Fluent readers

Step up your reading skills with playful narratives, new words and fun facts.

Middle Primary – Curious readers

Discover your world through science and stories.

Upper Primary – Adventurous readers

Explore your world through science and stories.

Climate Change: Wildfires

First published 2024

Published by Library For All Ltd
Email: info@libraryforall.org
URL: libraryforall.org

This project was delivered with the support of QBE under the Community Ready partnership.

Community
Ready

This book was made possible with the support of the Queensland Indigenous Land and Sea Ranger Program to support educational outcomes for children in Australia by learning from Indigenous knowledge and stewardship of Country. To learn more, visit https://www.qld.gov.au/environment/plants-animals/conservation/community/land-sea-rangers/locations.

Our Yarning logo design by Jason Lee, Bidjipidji Art

Climate Change: Wildfires
Williams, Clinton
ISBN: 978-1-923207-68-4
SKU04438